A GUIDE FOR THE PERPLEXED

The Omnibus Reader

by,

WILLIAM SCOTT MILLER

A GUIDE FOR THE PERPLEXED

<u>The Omnibus Reader</u>

OMP

Old Methodist Press
Oakland, California

Illustration: Hagenbeck-Wallace: Aerial Acts. 1922. Via Ringling- public domain.

This book is dedicated

to

Thomas Merton

INTRODUCTION

The title *A GUIDE FOR THE PERPLEXED* was inspired by Maimonides' text from 1190. In my own example, perplexed is both the reader's understanding of this work and our own journey into theology itself. A visual metaphor comes to mind, that of the two faced god Janus. A different face but of the same being, looking out over passageways.

Who is this Janus? Today we might describe him as a shape-shifter. I provide an example in my novella *THE OLD SEMINARY GHOST*. Yet the real shape-shifters are you and I. We constantly evolve and change our appearance, both inwardly and outwardly.

That journey is both intrinsic and extrinsic. To borrow another title from literature, *THE WIND IN THE WILLOWS* (Kenneth Grahame) the *Omnibus Reader* is that very wind. As for the willows- you will have to read *NOAH'S RAVEN: A Midrash Aggadah* to locate its place in Eden.

Omnibus Reader in this case simply refers to the literary work completed when I was in seminary. The purpose of this introduction is to give the reader some depth of field of the written work. What the reader will find here are descriptions of the work and one example from each text. That also seems to be the task of all of us in theology, even the likes of myself on the creative end of the bookshelf.

There are theologians I cannot live without and crave like fine chocolates. Yet my true brothers are the likes of Kerouac and Ginsberg, rebel theologians from on and off the road. I encourage you to search out the chocolates. What I provide is something to read while you savor them.

Of the work itself there are two books I wish to highlight for the reader. The first is *LECTIO DIVINA: Advent to Pentecost.* The liturgies are driven by our narrator Guillaume and his partner

Marcel. Each Sunday they experience a hierophany together. Then they encounter the strange and delightful Winter Marionette Theater, whose performances follow the Revised Common Lectionary. The Winter Marionette Theater had been driven from their home in Paradise California, by the fire that destroyed that town. They barely escaped in their truck, which was full of their marionettes, costumes and musical instruments. It is during Lent that we find Ariadnie, the director of the Winter Marionette Theater, returning to Paradise. She does so by entering into the world of the dead, as she visits the victims of the fire.

The *FEAST OF SAINT IGNATIUS: An Ignatian Meditation* uses the Examen Prayer. I call this a pentatonic paradigm. It has five parts, think of them as notes of music, they are used for individual spiritual assessment and also as a spiritual exercise. I use them as a spiritual assessment in my work as a hospice chaplain or in spiritual direction. Consider using this prayer as your own daily meditation.

This *Omnibus Reader* is of course its own feast, the feast of that exacting spiritual hunger, which is fed by fire. The fire is always a phoenix. You will find that phoenix in the last chapter of *Advent to Pentecost*, as the Firebird.

LECTIO DIVINA: Sundays after Pentecost
&
LECTIO DIVINA: Advent to Pentecost

*LECTIO DIVINA: Sundays after Pentecost &
Advent to Pentecost* are for the practice of lectio
divina and contain my original litanies and
canticles, celebrating an entire liturgical year. They
are appropriate for use in a group study and styled
for worship.

Sundays after Pentecost and *Advent to
Pentecost* are different stylistically. *Sundays after
Pentecost* relies upon poetry as its medium and has
a focus on social justice with contemporary issues.

Advent to Pentecost relies upon storytelling.
In that we have recurring characters, which includes
the Winter Marionette Theater and its various
performers- human and otherwise.

Our example for *Sundays after Pentecost* is
a liturgy, lifting up Claudia Patricia Gómez
González who was murdered by ICE.

Second Sunday after Pentecost

<u>CALL TO PRAYER</u>

Peace be with you.

And also with your spirit.

<u>READING of the SCRIPTURE</u>

Psalm 5:1-3, NIV (note: deviation from lectionary)

The word of the Lord.

Thanks be to God.

<u>LITANY for CLAUDIA</u>

In the morning,

LORD, you hear my voice; in the morning*

*I lay my requests before you**

*And wait expectantly, **

In the morning, Lord*

In the morning.[1] Amen

CANTICLE for CLAUDIA

How can it be Lord?

That I a young woman,

Am shot dead by ICE.

Shot in the head,

I lay my requests before you[2]

The screaming,

My companions helpless and unarmed

My thoughts were of rest, of water

Living into my baptism, searching for refuge.

Do you hear my voice in the morning*

I lay my requests before you,[3]

Inscribed on my heart,

On my lips,

On my forehead now shattered

---

[1] Psalm 5:3, NIV
[2] Psalm 5:3b, NIV
[3] Psalm 5:3b, NIV

That place where I made the cross.

I lay my requests before you

And wait expectantly,

With the profound patience of the dead.

Too young to be a mother,

Too old to be a child

Too alive to be forgotten.

My companions will speak my name

Claudia Patricia Gómez González

My request is to be remembered

I am your daughter, Claudia

I lay my requests before you*

In the morning Lord,*

In the morning.[4]

<u>THE REFRAIN</u>

I am your daughter, Claudi;

I lay my requests before you

In the morning Lord, in the morning.

---

[4] Psalm 5:3, NIV

THE LORD'S PRAYER

Amen

LECTIO DIVINA

Scripture, Litany, Canticle, Refrain

DISMISSAL

Our next example moves to storytelling. Here we have Guillaume narrating as he and Marcel visit Old John of Carmel.

LECTIO DIVINA

Advent to Pentecost

First Sunday After Christmas Day

<u>CALL TO PRAYER</u>

Peace be with you.

> *And also with your spirit.*

<u>READING of the SCRIPTURE</u>

Psalm 148, NRSV

The word of the Lord.

> *Thanks be to God.*

<u>LITANY for the SEA MONSTERS</u>

Gracious God,

> *Your creation keeps us in awe,*

Just as we hear the ocean,

Tremble and roar so close to us, here

In this quiet town of Carmel

Where your aged son

Is amusing the children

For he likes them brought to him,

As they delight in your world,

As we do,

In theirs. Amen

CANTICLE for the SEA MONSTERS
On the first Sunday

After Christmas Day,

Old John rested

And his house was full of visitors,

Of whom he favored Ricardo

Who asked about the sea monsters.

And Old John felt he was blessed

By the presence of Ricardo

By his curiosity, his sense of wonder

But particularly his awe.

Visitors often inspected his yule tree,

For it had the most unusual ornaments-

Of these, Ricardo who was four

Had many questions.

Old John's tree had ornaments and lights,

But also sea monsters,

The creature of the Black Lagoon,

Mermaids, Mermen,

Animals too,

The cows, sheep of the manger,

But also orangutans, the wild boar

And over the years people brought him more:

Snakes and lizards, the creeping things

Hawks and cardinals, the flying things

And Chewbacca, who Ricardo pointed to

Asking why?

And Old John stood there

Holding his visitors rapt attention:

"Praise the LORD from the earth*,

You sea monsters and all deeps,[5]

Wild animals and all cattle,*

---

[5] Psalm 148:7,NRSV

Creeping things and flying birds!"[6]

Young men and women alike,*

Old and young together![7]

Could see how the tree's ornaments grew

Each era had its representatives

And Ricardo handed Old John a gift,

To put on the tree,

And John held it aloft and they cheered

For it was Ruth Bader Ginsburg,

And Old John said:

 "There was a judge named Ruth."

Old John placed it at the top,

By the angel, and proclaimed:

"Praise him, all his angels;*

Praise him, all his host!"[8]

And Ricardo said: "Amen."

And the people said: "Amen."

---

[6] Psalm 148:10, NRSV
[7] Psalm 148:12, NRSV
[8] Psalm 148:2, NRSV

<u>THE REFRAIN</u>

"Praise the LORD from the earth,*

You sea monsters and all deeps,[9]

*Wild animals and all cattle,**

Creeping things and flying birds![10]

Gracious God,

Your creation keeps us in awe,

<u>THE LORD'S PRAYER</u>

Amen

<u>LECTIO DIVINA</u>

Scripture, Litany, Canticle, Refrain

<u>DISMISSAL</u>

---

[9] Psalm 148:7, NRSV
[10] Psalm 148:10, NRSV

STRANGE MINISTRATIONS

A Seminarian's Journal

STRANGE MINISTRATIONS: A Seminarian's Journal contains the following: contemporary prayers, rites, liturgies, meditations, celebrations, feast days, memorials and sermons. It also includes a reflection (below) on my visit to Saint Louis for the rather ugly tussle with homophobia in the Methodist Church. It concludes with an essay on the history of racism within Methodist history and how homophobia has simply supplanted institutionalized racism.

SAINT LOUIS BLUES

I was at the Blues Museum of America in Saint Louis when I heard a familiar tune. It was "I been down so long," Bob Kirkpatrick was singing. I followed the music and found the source. There was a black and white photograph of the guys. The year posted on the photograph was 1973. Outside it was a bitter cold February day and I was taking a break from the so-called Special Session of the General Conference of the United Methodist Church. The purpose of which was to vote on the fate of queer clergy and the rights of LGBTQi members.

I was there as a seminarian from the left side of the church. Well Berkeley is on the left coast. It is also warmer there. That we were there at all seemed bizarre. I was asked by my polite Lyft drivers why I was in Saint Louis and after I told them, they universally had the same reaction: "You're here to do what?" They were flabbergasted. This informal poll of mine was buoyed by the same comment of the friendly and uniformly African American wait help behind the counter at the concession stand at the conference center: "What?" That we were breaking bread with these hate mongering sycophants made me sick. Apparently the "help" shared in the sickness and had quickly sorted out reality from pretense.

In fact I was sick and ended up spending one morning in the hospital. My wife had warned me not to go on this trip but being a Midwesterner of stern Scottish stuff, I went. I regretted it except that I enjoyed being there. It was like a trip into the Gotham of Batman.

I am not a fan of Batman though some of my gay friends cannot resist it. I know the comics but have not seen the films. Nonetheless, I have an idea of the art direction and it rather fascinates me. It is a world George Grosz could have illustrated- at least the characters at the conference on the dais. But it is the city scape that lured me with its buildings, those vacant silhouettes that resonate with the inner meaning of the place. Saint Louis is that place of Midwestern emptincss. That emptiness and loneliness it connotes, can be located in its many vacant buildings, particularly downtown and along its vast stretch of boarded up brick homes and flats.

Blocks of them. It gives it an eerie Hitchcock touch-where evil lingers in daylight and ruffles its plumes by night.

After I decamped from the hospital I returned to the arena, my name for the conference center which had once been the home for the NFL Cardinal football team. The concessions counter there was seemingly unchanged. So was the fare. Bland, heart clogging stuff with the kind of coffee fit for a styrofoam cup. Not surprisingly the signs for beer were taped over but you could still see the message underneath: Beer! I took it as an omen, the leaders of the church had taped over what could not be seen or said, much less tasted. The conservatives were here to tape over, indeed to drive the nails in the coffin, of my rainbow garbed associates.

For a huge gathering of Methodists, those folks known for worshiping in the great outdoors, this event with its artificial lights, artifice and deal

mongering fix was part nightmare and part mystery.
How did we get there? Its mix of Robert Rules of
Order and praise music would have inspired Dali or
Buñuel. These were strange ministrations indeed.

The rules of order seemed tailor fit for the banality
of evil while the praise music was fit for a madman.
What were they praising? Now it seemed as if
divine intervention had given me a perspective on
this obnoxious song and dance routine- swaying and
praying. Where was Bob Kirkpatrick? But that
would mean the event had a soul, a soul that was
sick but still could sing and swing. I've been down
so long it looks like up to me.
Meanwhile one of my trans friends was in the lobby
with her sign: your chance to talk to a queer person.
An African bishop was talking with her when the
two of us met. She is a classmate of mine. No
sooner had I stopped than a reporter from the St.
Louis Post Dispatch and a photographer were at her
side, they wanted her story. That afternoon a picture

of her with the African bishop was on CNN and the story appeared in papers everywhere. Celebrity. The African delegates voted overwhelming to say no to queer rights and keep Methodist apartheid alive. There were stories of vote buying, undue influence and the like at the conference. Later these stories bore fruit. But I went there knowing the fix was in. After all, I grew up in Chicago. It was a dirty business.

I escaped to find some real coffee. I was still transfixed by Bob Kirkpatrick but began to think more of Leonard Cohan and his song Hallelujah. It is a song where we think praise but it is really one of lament for lost faith. I had brought along a biography about him for my trip but I was too sick to read it, sleeping when I should have been reading. The picture I had of Gotham also began to change. Now I thought the illustrator should be Ralph Steadman. Fear and Loathing in Saint Louis?

The seminarians packed their bags and left. I lingered a bit before my flight. I had not been back in the Midwest in over thirty years. I enjoyed the brisk walks downtown and the friendly people. I was also curious about the vacant buildings.

Spring came, graduation from seminary and writing a book during the summer, but I kept note of Saint Louis. In a bizarre turn of events there has been a string of child murders in the African American community. All of them are unsolved. In my own mind I considered it in the wake of this ugly event in Methodist history, now forgotten (if ever considered) by the locals. We progressive Methodists turned our attention to immigration and the environment. No word however about the fate of the people in Saint Louis. Only from one friend of mine, a Jesuit on Holy Hill, did I hear of a plan for social action in Saint Louis. I thought this was very curious. We were so busy with our agenda we did not see the people around us.

This left me thinking, what is the evil that lurks?

Methodism began as a social movement within the Church of England. It seems at its best when strapped to the lexicon of praxis. Its blind spot appears to be the contemplative tradition and spirituality in tandem with social change. My friend the Jesuit got this. Methodism is a ship grounded on the rocks with its passengers fighting over the lifeboats. The band plays on like on the Titanic. But which band and what music?

In my essay that follows this reflection, I quote the writer Randy L. Maddox, how "Eastern Christians believe how we in the west reduce sacraments to merely certifications of juridical pardon." My own take on the conservative Methodists who are clearly bigots, is that they mistake "Wesley's distinctive soteriological concerns (responsible grace and therapeutic salvation) within the categories of guilt

and merit (Maddox). " Those of us here on the
theological edge- the left coast which may or not be
geographical, have more experience with Zen and
non-duality. These are ideas foriegn to our
counterparts. It is a ground of being that
acknowledges the creation as interconnected and
that we are stewards of the earth, not its exploiters.
But this paradigm I fear reads as too pat, too smug,
even if I agree with it.

There is a more complex phenomena here and it's
the role individuation has in our religious life. There
is an insight here by Carl Jung, from *The
Psychology of Kundalini Yoga*, Pages 39-40, that
unwraps it: "Individuation is not that you become
an ego—you would then become an individualist.
You know, an individualist is a man who did not
succeed in individuating; hc is a philosophically
distilled egotist."

For me this is the difference in letting go of a juridical soteriology for a transformative completion of one's soul. The purpose here should be obvious, we peel back the ego to reveal the self. That's what scares the crap out of the conservatives.

I went to seminary after I retired. My perspective is logically somewhat different than the younger students. This goes for my peers who are my age for I am less vested in what happens to the church, it's pension and jobs. I deeply admire my progressive friends, particularly queer clergy who have thrown down the gauntlet, come what may. They have guts and the courage of their convictions.

I am a spiritual director, a writer and volunteer hospital chaplain. Tomorrow I will return to the hospital and the concerns about theodicy among the patients. I no longer care about the Methodist schism. The seeds for its dissolution were sown long ago with accepting slavery and then segregating their black congregations. Let the movement continue but let this church die.

My thoughts are with the people of Saint Louis, their vacant houses and buildings and how systematic evil is present in their lives and ours. I care too for the emptiness and loneliness which I believe is pervasive in this weird and cruel Methodism that the conservatives have unleashed. How small their lives are when the riches of God's splendor are at their doorstep.

Looking across the expanse of Methodist history I see a struggle against that evil. That struggle goes on today in many Methodist Churches. But I also see great complicity and compromise. Leonard Cohen move over, I am with you.

THE OLD SEMINARY GHOST

THE OLD SEMINARY GHOST is a novella that
uses its light touch to explore our questions on
eschatology and loss. The ghost may or not be
Henry James, Sr. who does not believe in ghosts.
The intended audience for this book is a reading
group close to All Souls Day. Below we have the
first chapter- you may want to join them for coffee.

Tête-à-Tête

Professor Ashendon had a most perplexing

problem. What to do when the seminary ghost

retires? Other retirements offered the usual

conventional challenges: tepid farewells, garrulous

speeches by the honoree- often the propelling

reason for much celebration and then the gut

wrenching animus over emeritus status. This last

was a most touchy subject. As dean he had been blessed with a faculty without the clueless example who sought this designation, unlike some of the other seminaries here on Holy Hill. One unnamed seminary nearby offered emeritus status to all their retired faculty. Old Seminary, his institution refused to bend to this altruistic rod. So it was with much pleasure that he offered this distinction to the seminary ghost. Which now brought him here to the Uplift Cafe on Euclid Avenue. For the ghost not only refused but brusquely waived off the farewell party.

Boris Godunov entered the cafe in his Boris-like manner. He bored in. Small of stature yet large in profile, he exudes the confidence of a raven in his guile and cunning. His jet black hair and eyes gave him the appearance of a newly discovered silent film star. Always dressed in black, today he was wearing a black fedora, which made him look like a pal of Edward G. Robinson. Boris, the former aspiring Dominican, was now the director of the academically suspect but popular Institute of Demonology. He was a popular fellow among seminarians. These he greeted with his customary aplomb, waving to them like the pope as he brought his cappucino to Professor Ashendon's table. "Peace be with you Ralph."

"And also with you Boris." Professor Ashendon watched as Boris removed the fedora, stroked his mane of hair into place, setting his glinty eyes upon him. It was always like this, he thought, the stage drama and now the dressing table habit.

The two old friends sat at the back of the cafe. Boris facing him and he looking out toward the street. Everywhere students had their laptops, alone with their work or chatting with friends. It all seemed so normal he thought, only it was not.

"Your thoughts my friend?" Boris was concerned. Professor Ashendon was looking old. Indeed they were both old and seemed older still in this milieu. He watched Professor Ashendon pull on his now white beard and remembered when it was hazel brown. He could still see the color in his eye brows despite Professor Ashendon's glasses. His hair, unlike that of Boris, had disappeared with the years, leaving just a few tufts above and below. Sign posts of another age.

"I need your help, old man."

"Personal or professional?"

"Personnel actually." He wasn't actually sure how he was going to present his problem to Boris. By admitting that there was a ghost at Old Seminary he would be validating Boris' position that ghosts did indeed exist. "You see, we have a problem with a ghost." There he put it out. What else could he do?

"Old James eh?" Boris said with a glimmer of both humor and concern.

"Good God man, you mean to say you know? Well," pausing for a moment looking out to the sidewalk, "there have always been rumors."

"You forgot I taught at Old Seminary last year. And to put your mind right, yes. Many people know these rumors. Most of the students here in the cafe have heard the rumors. After all, what is a seminary without a ghost?" Boris chose his words carefully and spoke slowly, unlike his usual bullet approach. He wanted to make sure Professor Ashendon heard him.

"I confess I am betwixt and between. On the one hand, it has been a financial benefit having this rumor about the seminary being haunted. It has increased enrollment. On the other, on the other…"

"It's a problem when it is not just a rumor or legend. That it is real." Boris finishing Professor Ashendon's thought for him.

"Yes. Something like that." Professor Ashendon had long since finished the blueberry scone he was eating and was now folding his napkin in quarters, till he could fold no more. "You see I met him."

"Henry James, Sr.?"

"Cantankerous fellow, though very nice to me." And in saying these words suppressed his delight but also frustration that Boris knew his identity.

"What was it like?"

"I was upstairs in Huntington Hall when this fellow passed me and said good evening. He was rather chipper and had a purposeful manner. He was also carrying a book."

"What else?" Boris now the interviewer, knowing this is why his friend had asked to meet, that Boris would take things into hand.

"My mind was on other things, my '47 Ford actually."

Boris smiled. His friend was revealing his one true love and passion which is reserved for old cars. He had ridden in Professor Ashendon's spotless black '47 Ford just recently. His friend had even smoked a cigar while he smoked a joint. After all, it was legal now. "So you were distracted."

"Yes. Then it hit me. Dressed as if it were 1850, the cravat and that strange beard men affected then, grown under the chin and oddly on the neck. Bald pate, strong expression and hearty demeanor."

"Any other telling details?" Boris the noir detective.

"Hmm," Professor Ashendon now smiled. "You know what it is. The limp. James was an amputee."

"Correct!" This elicited an uproarious and unexpected laugh from Boris.

Until now the other cafe patrons had largely ignored them although heads always turned toward Boris. Professor Ashendon thought he might have suddenly become in their eyes, an unwitting raconteur. It was a sobriquet he had never earned and indeed he had willingly given up sermons because they were exasperatingly didactic. "I suspect old man that my description has hit a nerve of familiarity."

"Indubitably so. To the tee as they say. Except my experience was somewhat more in duration."

"How so?" sounding curious and now putting his squared off napkin in his coffee mug, an exercise he had been doing for the past thirty years.

"I responded to the good evening with my own. I knew who he was immediately, although frankly I could hardly believe it. Perhaps a joker? An eccentric colleague of yours?"

"We have those, you are one of them."

Ignoring this, "I said good evening Mr. James, it is so nice to meet you."

"And he said?" Professor Ashendon asked with some urgency and a bit of pique, why had he not been so quick on his feet?

"Before I could introduce myself he said:
'Boris Godunov, my pleasure. Any man named
after an opera is a friend of mine. Now if you will
excuse me, I have an urgent appointment
downstairs.'" He looked at his friend who was
taking this in and continued, "and with that he lit
out of there downstairs."

"The artificial limb doesn't seem to hinder
his walking."

"Ghosts are like that. Now tell me Ralph
because I'm dying to know, is this your only
encounter with James?"

"No not at all. We have spoken often either
in my office and at home. He likes my digs as I
have a fireplace. You recall his familiar phrase: 'I
love the fireside rather than the forum?'

"Yes he is the master of the sitting room discussion. Broadsides really if Henry David Thoreau is to be believed. What happens to him, I mean after the two of you have your tête-à-tête?"

"He sleeps in my spare bedroom, although I rarely see him in the morning. When I open the door he is usually gone."

"I see. Are these office visits awkward?"

Sensing the direction of the question Professor Ashendon shifted on his chair, pausing before he answered. "At first I played opera during our discussions. I was afraid someone in the hallway might think I was just talking to myself. One day I forgot to turn the music on and there was a knocking at my door."

"A rat tap tapping?"

"Yes but not the raven. I opened the door and it was a student who had an appointment. To my surprise, James did not disappear. He does that sometimes and I envy him, so many times I wish I could do the same. Instead James got up, welcomed the student in and excused himself."

"Ralph, did the student think anything was amis? Like who was this gentleman from another time?"

"No, students don't notice things like that. I suppose he thought James was just a doddering old colleague of mine."

"I should tell you Ralph that I too have had several conversations with your man James."

"I am not surprised. You see all the faculty have including the staff. Some get it and others don't. One golden rule though is observed, no one talks about it openly. They just say that they have seen the ghost."

"Ah yes. So tell me now what is the problem. It sounds like having the ghost of James has been more of a benefit than a problem."

"Exactly my friend, that is precisely the case. You see he wants to move on. We have gotten used to him but he not us. I'm afraid we exasperated him despite our having Swedenborgian faculty. He tells me that he is being called to a church in San Francisco. I have offered to host a retirement party for him and even make him an emeritus faculty member, but to no avail."

Boris who is surprised by little was now surprised by a lot. He had always admired Professor

Ashendon who was a biblical scholar, a self described generalist and linguist. He had his passions and became an authority on the Clementine Homilies and their characters, Nicetas and Aquila in particular. James was a new passion. Another surprise was Professor Ashendon sharing with him a paper he had written on Ralph Waldo Emerson. A subject far afield from Nicetas and Aquila. To Boris' amazement it was a page turner, as if Professor Ashendon had actually been there with Emerson. Now he knew he had. Through James!

His friend was also a decent bloke and good dean, a fair administrator in a world of big fish in small ponds. He could see why James had taken a liking to him. It was also beginning to become apparent why his friend needed his help. "So you want me to help you replace James?"

"Yes. I don't know why I couldn't just come out and say it. We need a new seminary ghost."

NOAH'S RAVEN

<u>*A Midrash Aggadah*</u>

NOAH'S RAVEN: *A Midrash Aggadah* is a novella that tells the end of the Noah story from the point of view of the Raven. This midrash uses Mesopotamian mythology, particularly that of the Gilgamesh epic and its character Utnapishtim. Another influence has been the Babylonian Talmud: Tractate Sanhedrin Folio 108a. Most readers will see this as a fable or similar to *The Chronicles of Narnia*. The audience for this book is a reading group. Below is the introductory chapter.

<u>A Tiny Ship</u>

At the end of forty days Noah opened the window of the ark that he had made and sent forth a raven. It went to and fro until the waters were dried up from the earth. Genesis 8:6-7

After each passage of the water below, Orion the Raven alighted upon the ark. Unbeknownst to Noah, whom Orion suspected of having a passionate desire for Mrs. Raven, he nourished himself and rested. Astir assured her mate, that she had thwarted the over attentive Noah with a few finely delivered pecks. Orion then bid his wife Asitr farewell and continued on his journey.

This journey lasted seven days and each day Orion pushed himself to fly farther in his circumnavigation of the ark. This endless and silent sea below him had no obvious sea marks, those odd undulations of waves that posit position by what lays below the surface. Orion had taken Asitir's advice in counting his wing flaps, much like a man counting steps in the snow when lost in the mountains. In this manner he mathematically created his own navigation system over the mirror blue sea. Just when he could push himself no farther and about to turn back, he spotted something floating on the surface below.

It was a craft of sorts that appeared to be fashioned from cedar logs. It's detail became more apparent the closer he flew to it. It was in fact a catamaran with a cabin on its cross beam, a wheel which he later learned was for navigation and a mast with a square white sail. Today the sail and its long pennant above was slack for lack of wind. Orion noted that the pennant was purple with blue crosses. Upon closer inspection he saw that the entire vessel had been decoratively carved with geometric patterns. He could only discern one figurative symbol, that of the ouroboros, the snake that consumes its tail. The two cedar logs, wide at the stern were tapered toward the bow, tipped with copper. Unlike the crude ark this was a vessel of particular design besides being one of great fortitude. What astounded Orion was that he was looking at a miniature craft!

As he alighted upon it he found how tiny it was. No human being could possibly use it, except as a toy. Perhaps it was the gift of a prince to his son cast adrift during the flood. He paused to rest, glad for the moment to gather his senses before he had to return to the dismal prospect of the ark. Just as he was about to fly off he was startled by something behind him.

For there stood a man holding a spear the size of a toothpick. If such a being could be called a man. A man who measured no more than two inches tall. Orion realized that he must appear huge and frightful to this odd but seemingly nonchalant creature. The tiny man appeared much unlike Noah and his scruffy family. This tiny fellow had a warm countenance, blue eyes that sang when you really saw them and an inviting manner. Yet he had so far not said a word. Or rushed away in panic! Orion took in his long white wispy beard that reached his waist, red conocular hat and purple clothes with white stripes.

"Greetings Raven," said the little but deep voice. You have nothing to fear and are welcome. It has been a long while since we have had company."

"We?" Orion found that a woman was now standing next to the man. She was wearing a green and lavender checked shawl and yellow dress.

"Greetings," said the woman. "You are welcome to rest here until you have to return to the ark."

"Perhaps introductions are in order," said the man, putting aside his spear. "The spear is only to ward off the leviathan. We do not fear you despite your reputation for eating the dead."

"Indeed," replied Orion. "It might be pointed out that man too only eats creatures that are dead. He seems to forget that obvious point when criticizing ravens. My name is Orion and my wife Astir is aboard the ark."

"I am Nicetas and this is my wife Aquila."
Aquila made a small curtsy to Orion. "Aquila,
perhaps you could go below and get some
nourishment for our guest?" And with that Aquilla
went below the hull leaving the two new friends
alone.

"I am mystified Nicetas. I confess I have
never seen a man such as you in all my days."

"That is our way Orion, we tend to keep out
of sight. We are also vegetarians and eat seeds, nuts
and berries much like many of your winged
cousins."

Aquila now came upon deck with a basket
of food.

"You will see friend Nicetas that I too enjoy
this simple fare." Orion then indulged his hunger,

for although he preferred the fallen flesh, he was faminished. "I greatly appreciate your hospitality Aquila."

"Please take something to your wife. I will go below to get it for you before you leave."

"Can you enlighten me sir where you are from? It must be from some far away place, at least far from where ravens fly and see the world."

Nicetas stroked his wispy beard for a moment wondering how to answer Orion. "We are descendents of the nephilim."

"The nephilim! But dear sir were they not giants?" Now Orion was truly perplexed. Perhaps he was dreaming, asleep back at the ark.

Nicetas chuckled. "Well we too think it is a strange irony. What I can share may be legendary but it is the history of our people. In ancient days there were two angels who were like brothers to each other. Both fell in love with mortal women and they bore them children. One was born on the fall equinox and the other on the spring equinox. Like the angels these women were dear friends but not sisters. Both prayed that their children would never be seen by mortal men, for they feared their offspring may be slayed. When their children were born their prayers were answered. The children were our size and could only be weaned by milk and honey. The first child was a boy and the second a girl. We bear their names. From them came generations of nephilim but only we have survived the great flood."

"Thanks to my husband's ingenuity!" his wife proudly proclaimed.

"I see that," said Orion, admiring the tiny vessel. "But tell me sir, surely your race has been harrassed by creatures great and small who might take you for their dinner. Or at least an appetiser?"

"No. Fortunately we have the blood of the nephilim in our veins. Small creatures and the great ones avoid us, they fear us and leave us alone."

"What about man?"

"This holds true for most humans as well but we believe that due to our human ancestry, some day they will accept us."

"I must return to the ark, although frankly I would not return except for my wife."

"Let me get you something you can take to her," said Aquila. And with that she returned to the hull to retrieve a basket for Astir.

"I don't know about trusting humankind Nicetas. But for myself I would like to return to visit you."

"You will always be welcome Orion."

Orion took the gift basket in his beak amazed at what he had encountered. It was too fantastic and he knew his wife would not believe it- except for the gift basket. As he flew toward the ark he saw a shadow in the water below it. It was the leviathan. It lay far below the ark following its movements. What does this portend he wondered? Concerned he decided not to share this with Astir.

He would return to see Nicetas, not just for his advice but also to warn him.

The next day Noah sent out the dove and the sea began to recede. Orion kept to his flying to avoid Noah and the day before land was sighted, he and Astir both flew to the tiny boat with their friendly crew. As before Orion alighted onto the tiny ship's forecastle, this time with Astir beside him. Nicetas and Aquila were there waiting for them.

"Welcome home my friend!" proclaimed Nicetas.

"Many thanks friend Nicetas. May I please introduce my wife Astir, this is Nicetas and his wife Aquila."

Nicetas gave a little bow to Astir while Aquila curtsied and said, "Our home is your home, always."

Astir noticed that they both wore a pendant of lapis lazuli. "What a beautiful pendant you are wearing."

"Many thanks Astir. My husband also has one. They were gifts from a noble patron long ago."

"Nicetas laughed. "Long ago in human years, beyond that of your captain Noah."

"That man, don't get me started," said Astir. He brought seven pairs of the so-called clean animals and just one pair of the unclean- meaning ravens. How can our species survive without a flock?"

“We might have a solution for you both,” replied Aquila.

“You see we are in the same predicament,” added Nicetas. “However we believe that the Mouth of the Rivers did not flood, there should be abundant life there including ravens and gnomes.”

“Gnomes?” both Orion and Astir asked at once.

“Yes,” it is what we are called though we are descendents of the nephilim. Gnome means gnostic as in a hidden wisdom.”

“Your wisdom is not hidden my friend,” said Orion. “Just look at this ship you have built.”

“Many thanks brother Raven. I plan on sailing there tonight. Perhaps the two of you would like to join us? We have sufficient provisions.”

"Yes please do," said Aquila encouragingly.
"There should be many ravens there and other
creatures both great and small."

"How is it they did not perish in the flood?"
Orion asked, not wanting to sound skeptical.

"They are the survivors of the previous
flood," said Nicetas. "Aquila will explain it to you
as she is the historian in the family."

Aquila raised her hands to fashion an oran,
opened her arms outward and began to speak. "In
another time there was a similar flood and a man
named Utnapishtim."

Aquila's green eyes began to sparkle and her
whole being now seemed particularly animated.
The ravens were solemn but entranced and even

Nicetas, who had heard the story many times was anticipating her words.

"Utnapishtim like Noah was given a task by the gods to build an ark, take the beasts, birds and all creepy crawly things with him. Then a great flood came and it rained for seven days and nights. His ark abbutted Mt. Nimush and there was a great clatter and moaning among the beasts. Then the birds flew and the creepy things crawled from the ark with great alacrity. The gods were divided about his great accomplishment. After a fiery discussion they anointed Utnapishtim and his wife, giving them eternal life. They bequeathed the Mouth of the Rivers as a place to reside for eternity."

Orion was flabbergasted at this tale. "Where is this Mouth of the Rivers and would not it flood, I mean given that it is in low land close by water?"

"It is located just East of Eden. Few have heard of this place but at one end there is a seraphim with a sword of fire where only Utnapishtim may pass."

"I have heard of this place from Noah and his children," said Astir. "But tell me, you say the gods found favor with Utnapishtim, is this the same God that spoke to Noah?"

"We believe," said Nicetas "that it is the same God. That this is a lost story and in the ancient days there were people, also like today, who believe there are many gods. Now there is more to the story, would you like to hear it?"

The ravens both nodded their heads wanting more. For Aquila's storytelling was a balm that soothed them from their wretched journey in the ark.

"There was a young and magnetic man named Gilgamesh who was full of folly, humor and bravery. After his companion died he was sorrowful and sought out Utnapishtim, who on learning this returned to Mt. Nimush. It was there that Gilgamesh met him and requested the secret to everlasting life. Utnapishtim gave him a task to stay awake for six days and seven nights promising that if he did he would provide for his wishes. However Gilgamesh promptly fell asleep and slept for six days and seven nights! Utnapishtim had his wife bake a loaf of bread each day to prove to him that the time had passed when he awoke. When he did he was crestfallen and defeated. Utnapishtim being generous and kind gave Gilgamesh a special secret for new life and vigor. He told him to gather the boxthorn plant at the bottom of the sea which he did. However on bringing it to land it was eaten by a snake, and this is why the snake sheds its skin like the moon sheds its shadow."

"And we," said Nicetus, "are in possession of this very boxthorn plant, which we will share with you."

The ravens were speechless.

"Your journey has been long," said Aquila, "just as ours was with Utnapishtim, but ours was not as long or arduous." Aquila then went into the hull to retrieve the plant for their guests.

"I would give anything to go to the Mouth of the Rivers," said Astir.

"I too," replied Orion, "though I am very curious as to the fate of Noah."

"Perhaps both can be accomplished," said Nicetas. "First you will need us to navigate you there and if you were to fly it would be too far a journey. However with the boxthorn plant you will retain all your resources and strength."

"Then it shall be done," said Orion sounded determined. "You shall fly on us tucked into our feathers."

"I too am curious about this Noah," said Nicetas, "as the same amount of time has now elapsed as it did for Utnapishtim."

"I see landfall ahead," said Aquila.

The ravens turned toward the ark which they had ignored since they landed, just when Aquila had returned with the boxthorn plant. For the ark had drifted and there was visible now a peak beyond it.

"That would be Mt. Ararat," said Aquila. "Here, take some of this and refresh yourselves. They did so and the ravens stirred with a force of new life. "Return to the ark and discover what will happen next. We will be here waiting for you. The water will recede and we will all be on land. Our ship will be easy to find with its white sail visible from the sky. Then we shall all travel to the Mouth of the River together."

"I should mention friend Nicetas," said Orion, "that on returning yesterday I saw what looked to be the leviathan lurking below the ark."

"This portends a bad omen," replied Nicetas.

"Possibly," said Aquila. "It is not dangerous as in a sea monster although that is what mankind believes. In reality it is a shadow."

"A shadow of the ark?" asked Asir.

"Not cast by the sun, rather a projection of something within the ark which would be an ominous foreboding. You have a special gift Orion to be able to see it."

The ravens said a fond farewell and took to the air with a vigour they had entirely forgotten. While their spirits soared their joy was tempered by the dark outline of the leviathan that shadowed the ark. Arriving, they flew into the window that had been their portal to the outer world. They had not been missed, for there was a clamor onboard. The journey for Noah and the animals was about to end.

Only how it would end was on Orion's mind. Badly

he thought but he kept these musings to himself.

MR. PARSONS' NOSE

A Comic Spiritual Journey in Light Verse

*MR. PARSON'S NOSE: A Comic Spiritual Journey
in Light Verse* tells the story of Mr. Parsons as he
explores the seven sacraments- or perhaps they
explore him. This book has a midrash in its last
chapter that helps the reader reframe what is
sacramental.

The audience for this book is general but it
is intended for young people. It is best read aloud in
a small group. This book was written prior to
attending seminary. It was reworked and published
again under a new name. It is also a homage to
Nikolai Gogol's story, *The Nose.*

Mr. Parsons' Baptism

When Mr. Parsons was baptized

It was really quite a scene,

For he bumped his nose

On the lip of the pool,

Leaving it looking rough and mean.

For he had a massive proboscis

Or perhaps a snout

It ruined his love life

Of that there can be no doubt

And when he looked in the mirror-

Oh my! It was so long!

And he cursed the heavens,

Because he knew it was wrong.

Poor Mr. Parsons

Had been a lonely chap

But after his submersion

We who came to know him

Began to see his conversion.

No longer on street corners

With the idlers who gathered there

Or chat with the crazy woman

Sitting in the sculpture pool,

Quite bare.

For now his nose was a normal length

It had healed

And he grew a little moustache

Indeed, he had panache!

Mr. Parsons knew

It was time for a change

And so he said goodbye

To the church of Crabby Old Ladies

Unadorned or plain

Who while polite,

Were really quite a pain.

Frankly he was keen

On a young lady attending St. Mark's

She was fair of countenance,

The demure Miss Lark.

For unbeknownst to his detection

Miss Lark had spied him,

Admiring his own reflection!

It was there in the gelato shop

It was as if he were demented,

He gazed and could not stop

"Oh my, I look so divine!"

Whispered the demure Miss Lark.

And though he was taken unawares

Mr. Parsons smiled,

Knowing she was playing a part.

And what's this?

Gelato on my moustache, he thought

-for his new accoutrement

Gave him dash!

"I've waited so long, you see…"

He opened with those words

And she alighted next to hm,

Like a magical bird,

And with her wings

They flew together

And became great friends,

Every moment was a beginning,

Never an end.

FEAST OF SAINT IGNATIUS

<u>An Ignatian Meditation</u>

This is a guided meditation using the elements of the Examen Prayer: awareness of God, gratitude, awareness of emotion, taking one feature of the day and praying upon it, and preparing for the journey tomorrow. Matsuo Bashō is our narrator and his oarsman is paddling you on a trip past the Edenic Island. Below the water the colorful carp recite poems of their great deeds and fantastic encounters. Join us so you will not have to journey alone.

<u>Gratitude</u>

Rest now into gratitude

Into that place where you can begin again,

Rest now into gratitude,

Where harms and hurts are no longer deeds

But just alabaster figures on an ancient vessel

Use it now to draw water and wine

Do not fret over the empty vessel

It has a purpose,

Simply to be filled.

The lone stranger, perhaps it is you

Is to be befriended.

The empty house, fill it with guests

Be welcoming

Be observant

Be faithful

Demonstrate gratitude, for life

For the passing of this parade

For the walk on the veranda after we come to shore

Listen again to the paddles,

To faint echoes of children,

Tugging at the day's play

Their mothers gathering them

Just as you were gathered

And the stories you will tell

Of colourful carp,

Their stange ministrations on your behalf

Of the poems they recited as you held yourself quiet

Of their great deeds

And fantastic encounters

With demons, gamblers, itinerant preachers

All below silent water stirring

As only silent water can be stirred

By you

Or the oarsman, with dilapidated hat

A dissolute looking fellow-

You never quite see his face

Mustachioed, a wispy beard,

Quietly speaking in Japanese

A man resembling a mentenome,

Clicking a beat with the oars

Like the steady sap of a fan.

Your eyes are heavy,

The sun and the balance of the day is in your body,

Yet all you feel is gratitude,

To let him row you now toward the embankment,

To the scuttle of others along the pier,

To welcoming murmurs of your comrades.

BAPTISMAL RITE for a DEAD CHILD

Baptism and the act of committal fuse this inner historical and the transcendent moment within one rite. It allows the family to begin to formulate their own eschatological understanding of what has taken place.

Unlike baptism alone, it does not use water for a blessing but oil for anointing. Where it takes place is in the hospital. The purpose is for healing the souls of those present and honoring that God has yoked the child who has departed.

Below are the concluding verses of the liturgy:

Let these drops of oil

    Be drops of mercy

Let these drops of oil

    Remind us to love God and our neighbor

Let these drops of oil

    Bind us with (first name) throughout eternity.

(First Name)

    I baptize you

In the name of the Creator,

    And of the Son,

    And of the Holy Spirit.

    Amen

Holy Spirit

    A Firebird dancing

    A Phoenix rising at sunset

    A morning sun lit across all our expectations.

Holy Spirit

    An orchestra tunes

    And is about to play

    All the measures of a life not lived.

Holy Spirit

    Your gentle caring hands

    Plant the seeds of God's garden

    So providence itself is never denied.

Spirit of Holiness, we call to you
>   Glory to your name!

(Gather the family together and have them hold hands)

Gracious and loving God
>   Your healing spirit flows,
A sweet gentle breeze
>   With hints of frankincense and myrrh
A balm, a scent
With the promise of new spring rain
>   Over those who mourn.

Honoring the mystery of creation
>   Honoring both pain and joy
Now veiled, in the paradox of beauty.
>   Let us then never forget
That we, are the wounded healers
>   And in healing others
>   We heal ourselves.

(Benediction)

Now beloved friends,

> In the name of the Creator

And the Son and the Holy Spirit

> Our Baptismal service is ended,

May you all find the peace that you seek

And may the steps you take,

> Be filled with grace.

> Amen